BURFURT
and the
Garbanzo Beans

written by
ROSIE AMAZING
(age 6)

illustrated by
ANDREEA TOGOE

Once upon a time, Burfurt was at the farmer's market. And do you know what he sold? Garbanzo Beans!

There were all kinds of garbanzo bean flavours. Peppermint, coffee, lollipop, milk, spicy, maple syrup, pancake flavour, rainbow ice-cream flavour, salad flavour and more!

Burfurt also sold mugs and jars filled with garbanzo beans. He sold garbanzo bean crafts, garbanzo bean sculptures, garbanzo beans on a stick and garbanzo bean popsicles! He sold everything! Sometimes the garbanzo beans sold out!

Bufurt had lots of friends at the farmer's market, and they sold stuff too! Skunky the skunk sold coffee. Mooshie moose sold pictures and frames. His koala friend Oscar sold groceries like fresh vegetables. His friend Marco the puppy sold samosas and tandoori chicken. His friend Chloe the cat sold cozy clothes and Robin the froglet sold jewelry. Circles the dinosaur sold carrots and peaches. And he also sold games and magnets. He had this new game called 'The Dino Hunt.'

Burfurt loved to be with all his friends at the farmer's market!

Back home, Tommy was asleep. When he woke up, he saw that a package had been delivered.

But then something weird happened...

A voice was coming from inside the box. The voice was talking about yummy peanuts and putting those yummy peanuts into jars.

Weird.

But then something ELSE weird happened.

Something TERRIBLE!

Back at the market, Burfurt's garbanzo beans were missing!

ALL OF THEM!

"Somebody stole my garbanzo beans!" Burfurt cried and meowed on the phone to Tommy.

"Weird," Tommy said. "Not as weird as this talking box though..."

Then Burfurt spotted a doggie.

"That doggie has my garbanzo beans!" Burfurt cried.

Burfurt's cries startled the doggie, and he dropped the beans all over the place.

"Aren't the garbanzo beans free?" asked the doggie.

"No, silly puppy," giggled Burfurt. "You're supposed to buy them at the farmer's market."

"Ooops."

"Why don't you meet me at the market tomorrow, puppy? Then you can buy some garbanzo beans for real."

The next morning the doggie went to the farmer's market. Burfurt prepared some garbanzo beans for the doggie in a cute, little jar.

The doggie kissed Burfurt.

But Tommy still couldn't figure out what was going on with that weird box.

And that's the story of Burfurt and the Garbanzo beans.

The End.

Annelid Press

Like Rosie's Books?

Support Rosie by leaving a positive review on Amazon or GoodReads.

 Keep up-to-date by following us on Instagram:

https://www.instagram.com/annelidpress/

Did you know that you can play the Dino Hunt game?

Check out Brainy Games' Dino Hunt: https://dinohunt.fun/

Copyright © 2023 by Annelid Press
ISBN: 978-1-990292-42-2

All rights reserved. Published by Annelid Press. No part of this publication may be reproduced, stored in a retrieval system or transmitted, in any form or by any means, without the prior written permission of Annelid Press.

www.ingramcontent.com/pod-product-compliance
Lightning Source LLC
Chambersburg PA
CBHW040035050426
42453CB00003B/118